D1263884

DRAMA:

WHAT IS HAPPENING

DRAMA:
WHAT IS HAPPENING

The Use of Dramatic Activities in the Teaching of English

BY JAMES MOFFETT

NATIONAL COUNCIL OF TEACHERS OF ENGLISH

CONSULTANT READERS

Arthur Eastman, University of Michigan

Alfred H. Grommon, Stanford University

COMMITTEE ON PUBLICATIONS

James R. Squire, NCTE Executive Secretary, *Chairman*

Robert M. Gorrell, University of Nevada

John C. Maxwell, Upper Midwest Regional Educational Laboratory

Walter J. Moore, University of Illinois

Enid M. Olson, NCTE Director of Publications

EDITORIAL SERVICES

Judith Fuller, National Council of Teachers of English

FOREWORD

At the Pittsburgh meeting of the Conference on English Education in April 1967, James Squire cautioned the profession that although great steps forward might be taken by such group efforts as N.D.E.A. institutes and curriculum study centers, the genius of the individual innovator must continually be fostered and his insights noted and responded to.

This book brings before the profession the ideas of one such individual. Mr. James Moffett, though buttressed by a grant from the Carnegie Corporation, has pursued singly a unified conception about composition and communication, literature and language learning. There is no implication that Mr. Moffett has found the "correct" conception about teaching these matters, but he appears to have found an intriguing one.

The familiar tripod of language, literature, and composition, of note in recent curriculum development, reflects the organization of college English departments and the divisions of the discipline they represent. The tripod does not—and does not pretend to—provide an integrative base for learning about one's own language. This is left to the learner or to his teacher or to the materials which the teacher uses.

The various curriculum centers have approached the matter of integration severally through thematic units; through focus on types or specific works of literature with composition and language study tangentially related; through seeing language as the core of study with literature and composition viewed as manifestations of language; or through seeing or participating in the process by which literature gets written.

Mr. Moffett in his several studies suggests another integrative idea: a continuum of direct discursive experience for the learner. In brief, his thesis is that one learns about language, literature, and composition in a coherent way by participating in the experience of creating discourse: writing plays and short stories, poems, and other forms; or acting, interpreting, and creating drama in diverse and realistic situations. The sequence of these creative experiences is related to the maturing student and to the program of literature.

In Mr. Moffett's conception, discourse should be arranged along a continuum (or a general movement), extending from the person as an inner-speaker (soliloquy) to a speaker-about-things (essay). This spatial-psychological structure thus provides a consistent rationale for both teaching the individual to compose and for organizing his experiences with the discourse of others (i.e., literature).

In the present volume, Mr. Moffett sets forth the thesis that involve-

v

ment of the student with drama in its many forms is a major and usually unexploited method for leading the inner-speaker more fully onto the "stage" whereby he becomes a speaker to others. The child immersed in babbling about himself and his surroundings later, in varying degree, verges toward the essayist who usually talks about remote things to a remote audience. The thesis of the present booklet rests on the assumption that dramatic interaction—doing things verbally in situations with other people—is the primary vehicle for developing thought and language.

Learning by doing can be, with unimaginative direction, little more than learning by imitation. The use of interaction as outlined by Mr. Moffett in these pages is sufficient protection from merely patterned performance. Dynamic creation of dialogue, for example, as a means of learning about discourse requires a continual experimentation with the means of incorporating new data into the flow of emerging ideas and probing the welter of alternative choices available to the speaker, be they linguistic, cognitive, affective, or physical choices as a way of communicating.

In his book Mr. Moffett has attempted to provide a unifying framework capable of encompassing a variety of elements germane to language study—transformational grammar, rhetoric, stylistics, genre study, semantics, psychological process of communication, and many more. That these are cast into a discussion of drama and, while retaining their own outlines as topics, blend and support the discussion of drama is testimony to the viability of Mr. Moffett's thesis about language learning.

While secondary teachers occasionally may be impatient with theory, there is much in these pages to attract, even if the reader sets himself only to quarrel with Mr. Moffett's ideas. The essay bears the stamp of the author's teaching experience in working with a variety of schools to test out his theories. Secondary school English teachers are usually familiar with drama as a subject of literary study but may find difficulty accepting Mr. Moffett's suggestions that dramatic *activity* is a useful and necessary part of instruction in language. Nonetheless the argument is made that drama has much to contribute, and the open-minded reader will find fruitful suggestions buttressed by persuasive justifications for greater use of dramatic interaction in the classroom. While Moffett shares the major goals of the English teacher, his belief is that teachers have failed to use the intrinsic interest of dramatics in reaching these goals.

JOHN C. MAXWELL, *Secondary Section Chairman*
NATIONAL COUNCIL OF TEACHERS OF ENGLISH

PREFACE

I would like to argue here that drama and speech are central to a language curriculum, not peripheral. They are base and essence, not specialties. I see drama as the matrix of all language activities, subsuming speech and engendering the varieties of writing and reading. But to regard it so is to reconceive it, to perceive in it the germinal ideas and actions of other language behavior.

In order to exploit for pedagogical purposes some similarities between theatrical and everyday drama, I am going to set shuttling some two-way metaphors between them. That is, I will speak broadly and use ambiguously both the word *drama* and some other terms that name its components. For the sake of possible stimulus value, I hope the reader will indulge my shifting reference without always explicitly signaling the shifts. My purpose is to make art and actuality illuminate each other. Some definite recommendations for teaching methods will follow this theoretical discussion.

I am very grateful to the following people for criticizing this manuscript for me: Courtney Cazden and Anita Rui of Harvard University; Elizabeth Cawein of Weeks Junior High School in Newton, Massachusetts; my fellow members of the Study Group in Drama of the Anglo-American Seminar in the Teaching of English (Dartmouth, 1966)—Douglas Barnes of the University of Leeds; Anthony Adams of the Crutchfield Comprehensive School, West Bromwich, England; Arthur Eastman of the University of Michigan; and Benjamin DeMott of Amherst.

For criticism of the section of this paper employing concepts from transformational grammar ("Dialogue"), I am much indebted to Wayne O'Neil of Harvard, Edward Klima of M.I.T., and John Mellon of Harvard. They are not to be held responsible, however, for my presentation and use of these concepts.

The study which formed the basis of the manuscript was made possible by funds granted by Carnegie Corporation of New York. The statements made and views expressed are solely the responsibility of the author.

JAMES MOFFETT
Research Associate in English
Harvard Graduate School of Education

CONTENTS

STAGE DRAMA AND STREET DRAMA

The script of a play is a transcription of what a spectator should see and hear. The spectator is a kind of sound camera who records the play, but because he is human, he records it in a discursive way. If his sensory recording were written down—the vocal sounds as dialogue and the rest as stage directions—it would roughly recapitulate the script (except for Shavian extravagances).

This same spectator could go out of the theater into the street, note down his sensations as he witnessed some action, and thereby create a script of his own. Drama does not have to be vocal, or even human; it might be a dumb show or a game among dogs. Drama is any raw phenomena as they are first being converted to information by some observer.

Although the action that takes place in a theater has been premeditated, it has fundamentally the same impact on the spectator as real-life events. True, *knowing* that the events are artifactual, not actual, gives the spectator a different mental set and alters somewhat his responses, but in viewing both, the spectator is coding events directly for himself; he is looking on, not hearing about. What we witness both onstage and outside comes to us unmediated by any other mind, unabstracted except by our own perceptual apparatus, undigested, unreported. One reason an author works in the dramatic medium is that he wants the deeds he has invented to hit us at the same "gut" level that actualities do.

A comparison with narrative may help. The action of a narrative is not ongoing, it *has* gone on; it is *reported* action. As such it is a résumé of some previous drama—summarized and abstracted *by somebody,* a reporter, narrator. Although grammar tells us that the difference between *what is happening* and *what happened* is a time difference, much more than time is involved. Tense is a relation of speaker to events: if the events are unrolling before his eyes—ongoing—they are being coded for the first time by someone who is *attending* them (or "assisting at" them, as the French say) and who is therefore in the same plane of reality as the act-ors. This is his point of view. His coding of events is a first-order abstraction. As a report of what happened, narrative is a second-order abstraction. Compare the sensory stream of someone watch-

1

ing a football game with the Sunday newspaper account of the same game. Narrative is a further abstraction of some observer's prior abstraction. What makes events past is reporting them. What makes events present is attending them. Whereas narrative summarizes drama, drama elaborates narrative. Consider a reviewer's recapitulation of a play performance, then a dramatization of a short story. Whether actual or artifactual, drama is *what is happening,* with all that this implies.

A play of course only pretends to be raw, unabstracted phenomena; actually it is a highly sophisticated conceptual creation. Characters, settings, words, and deeds are carefully selected and patterned. In fact, one essential difference between the theater and the street is this difference between order and randomness—which is another measure of abstraction. So in this sense a play is very abstract. Characters tend to be representative, the actions symbolic, the words and deeds significant. By selecting and shaping, the artist abstracts reality into forms that mean something to the audience. The impact of a play is dependent on some resonance between what is happening on stage and what has happened in the life of the spectator. No matter how far he is from being a king or from killing someone, the beholder of a revenge tragedy finds, for the feelings of betrayal and the murderous desire for quittance, some analogs in himself. The playwright invites generalization but does not generalize himself because he does not speak. In presenting what is happening he is implicitly saying what happens. This transferability is what we mean when we speak of the significance of a work.

Nevertheless, a play is not a novel, poem, biography, or essay. Despite its selectivity, conceptualization, and implicit generalization, it is an imitation of physical action and therefore still shows characteristics of the unabstracted phenomena it imitates; it is calculated to affect a spectator in much the same way a real-life drama does when he is confronted with it. And you don't have to know how to read to follow a play. You can't backtrack, because words and deeds move irreversibly in time. Reflection is held to a minimum, to "thinking on your feet," though of course you may reflect later in tranquillity as you do about real events. No guiding voice conducts you, plays host, summarizes and explains. (To offset this lack of interpreter, some playwrights may create a character who serves as a narrator or as a *raisonneur,* but note that to the extent such a character remains a *character,* and the play a drama, the result is merely to create a new level of unabstracted information.) Regardless of how cerebral a statement some character may utter, it is the behavioral utterance of the statement and not its content that makes a play dramatic. If the author wanted his audience to reflect more en route, or wanted to reflect for them, he would write in another form.

Drama is the most accessible form of literature for young and uneducated people. It is made up of action; and the verbal action is of a sort we all practice all the time. A kindergarten child or an older illiterate can soliloquize and converse, verbalize to himself and vocalize to others. No written symbols are required. Drama is primitive: not only does it hit us at the level of sensation, affect, and conditioned response, but it seems in all cultures to be virtually the first, if not the first, verbal art to come into being, because it is oral and behavioral and functional, evolving directly out of real-life activities, such as propitiating gods, making rain, and girding for war. Indeed, a number of modern trends, such as happenings and the anti-play, have exerted force to return drama to a communal actuality.

The components of a play may be divided into the verbal and nonverbal. What the spectator sees, or what he hears that is not vocal, is of course contained in the stage directions. These are objects and actions that might be referred to in speech, and indeed are often referred to by the speakers. But speech, though on the one hand merely another recordable action, is obviously a very special one because it is symbolic. Not only can it be referred to like other objects and actions, but it refers in turn to other things not perceptible to an observer—things offstage, inside the speakers, and on invisible levels of abstraction. The speech components of a play are *soliloquy, dialogue,* and *monologue*—addressing oneself, exchanging with others, and holding forth to others. The nature of each of these, and the relations among them, imply some very important things, I believe, for the teaching of discourse. I would like to examine each of these three speech components as phenomena of both the theater and real life.

SOLILOQUY

Though theatrical convention and necessity require that a soliloquy be voiced, it is supposed to be unuttered thoughts, self-verbalization. Soliloquizing is thinking. At least as early as Henri Bergson and William James, psychologists have suggested that thought is inner speech. The notion has been subscribed to since by the social psychologist George Herbert Mead and by an impressive roster of contemporary specialists in learning theory and child development that includes Piaget, Vygotsky, Luria, and Bruner. The general concept is that most of our thinking, the verbal part, is a kind of unvoiced conversation within oneself. After acquiring speech socially, through interaction with other people, the child begins to distinguish between the speech he utters for himself and the speech he utters for others. At first he voices aloud all speech, typically failing, in his egocentricity, to discriminate talking to himself and talking to another. Once he does discriminate, this early "egocentric speech" splits into internal and external discourse. Both are instrumental but have different functions: internal speech serves to process information as a guide to action; external speech serves to communicate. The earlier egocentric speech is a "thinking out loud," a running accompaniment to play and thus probably not distinguished by the child from his other bodily actions. Part of this patter is simply a verbal encoding of physical things, and part is planning and self-direction—all of which he later inhibits because it is not socially adaptive, and may even be socially detrimental if uttered aloud. In shunting some of his own speech underground, the child is in effect internalizing the words, forms, and ideas of other people, since he learned them by imitation and interaction (although it is probable that he acts on this material according to innate structures he was born with). Anyone can observe for himself some of the stages of this internalization. A child will tell himself aloud in perhaps his parents' exact words that "we should not touch the vase." Children thinking about a task can be seen to move their lips, so that an experienced lipreader can tell what they are thinking as they verbally mediate the task.

It is not generally acknowledged just how much the social medium of exchange and the chief instrument of thought are one and the same—

4

language. Outer and inner speech reciprocally determine each other; they are a serpent with its tail in its mouth. What needs emphasis, however, is the probability that thought is the internalization of social processes. For this emphasis I turn to George Herbert Mead.

> In reflective intelligence one thinks to act, and to act solely so that this action remains a part of a social process. Thinking becomes preparatory to social action. The very process of thinking is, of course, simply an inner conversation that goes on, but it is a conversation of gestures which in its completion implies the expression of that which one thinks to an audience. One separates the significance of what he is saying to others from the actual speech and gets it ready before saying it. He thinks it out and perhaps writes it in the form of a book; but it is still a part of social intercourse in which one is addressing other persons and at the same time addressing one's self, and in which one controls the address to other persons by the response made to one's own gesture. That the person should be responding to himself is necessary to the self, and it is this sort of social conduct which provides behavior within which that self appears. I know of no other form of behavior than the linguistic in which the individual is an object to himself, and, so far as I can see, the individual is not a self in the reflective sense unless he is an object to himself. It is this fact that gives a critical importance to communication, since this is a type of behavior in which the individual does so respond to himself.

> ·

> The unity and structure of the complete self reflects the unity and structure of the social process as a whole; and each of the elementary selves of which it is composed reflects the unity and structure of one of the various aspects of that process in which the individual is implicated. In other words, the various elementary selves which constitute, or are organized into, a complete self are the various aspects of the structure of that complete self answering to the various aspects of the structure of the social process as a whole; the structure of the complete self is thus a reflection of the complete social process. The organization and unification of a social group is identical with the organization and unification of any one of the selves arising within the social process in which that group is engaged or which it is carrying on.

> The phenomenon of dissociation of personality is caused by a breaking up of the complete, unitary self into the component selves of which it is composed, and which respectively correspond to different aspects of the social process in which the person is involved, and within which his complete or unitary self has arisen; these aspects being the different social groups to which he belongs within that process.[1]

If I understand Mead correctly, self and mind are social artifacts, and the constituents of the self mirror the constituents of society; thought

---

[1] George Herbert Mead, "Self" in *On Social Psychology: Selected Papers*, ed. Anselm Strauss (Chicago: University of Chicago Press, 1964), pp. 206, 208.

involves incorporating the roles and attitudes of others and addressing oneself internally as one would address another externally.

As inner conflict becomes more important in the plays of Shakespeare, the soliloquies become longer and more numerous. Compare those of Brutus and Hamlet. Reflected in Hamlet's soliloquies are various "voices" of his culture, society, class, and family—belief systems, attitudes, points of view, and roles. These could be personified and each assigned certain lines from his soliloquies, thus creating an external dialogue to prove Mead's point. Hamlet is full of voices, ghosts. So is Willy Loman. And so are we all. Consider what it means when we say "I keep telling myself . . . ," "I debated with myself . . . ," "I talked myself into . . . ," and so on. Biologically each of us is a whole; only cognitively and culturally can we be split into speaker and listener.

To consider the same issue in reversal, the whole of a play may be considered as a soliloquy by the playwright, who is ventriloquizing. A playwright says what he has to say not through a monologue but through a colloquy of created voices. The ensemble of these voices externalizes his mind. This kind of ventriloquizing amounts to fractionating the total voice production of which he is capable, to breaking down his self into the many points of view, attitudes, and roles which actually and potentially comprise it. The failure of young readers to appreciate Dickens' caricatures, and the failure of critics to "understand" *Waiting for Godot,* stems from an insistence that each character be a whole person instead of recognizing that the dramatis personae are a whole person and that the characters are embodied tendencies and potentialities of that person. Becket's Gogo and Didi, Pozzo and Lucky are components of personality, paired. If a play works, communicates, it is because the same social forces that have installed voices in the author have also installed them in the spectator. Whether the playwright is sociological like Shaw, psychological like Strindberg, or both like Arthur Miller, their characters tend to speak as both personality components and as social forces. In *After the Fall* Miller finally completed a technical innovation begun by O'Neill in *Emperor Jones,* Tennessee Williams in *The Glass Menagerie,* and himself in *Death of a Salesman;* by exploiting the incorporation process for the very form of his play, he made the stage a peopled head.

To place the discourse of the individual in a perspective that helps us to contemplate it most usefully, let us imagine a set of concentric circles (see Figure 1) that has the individual as center. Each circle is a determining context for the smaller circles it contains, and therefore it governs them. "Larger" means "more universal." The largest or most universal context is the biological; that is, the structure of our nervous

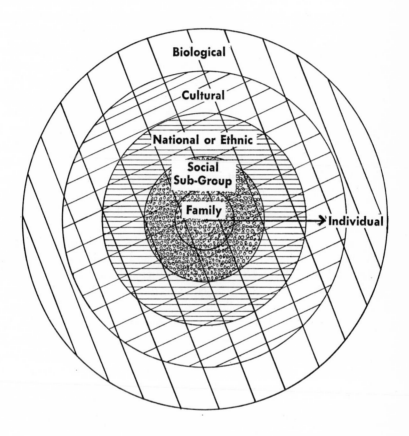

Concentric Contexts Determining the Individual's Language
FIGURE 1

system is what admits of the least individual variation, and the characterization of more localized contexts will be some more or less direct translation of man's biological being. If something innate explains language acquisition, as linguists of Noam Chomsky's persuasion believe, it is governed by this context. My own persuasion is that the predispositions for uniquely human kinds of abstraction are indeed innate, but not as "ideas," as Chomsky would have it. "Language universals," structures found in all languages, are probably reflections of neural structures as suggested by Warren McCulloch, for example.[2]

The next largest circle is the culture, which determines the thought of the individual through belief systems and postulates about nature built into its languages and supporting institutions. Within this context lie the cognitive differences among, say, Indo-European, Chinese, Eskimo, and Hopi cultures such as Benjamin Lee Whorf talked about. Though much disputed, Whorf's hypothesis that the categories and grammar of a particular culture shape the thought of the individual is bound to be *relatively* true. What is an open issue is the proportionate influence on the individual of language universals on the one hand and cultural idiosyncrasies on the other—the relative weight of the innate and the acquired.

But this issue is complicated tremendously by the influence of the successively smaller contexts—the national and ethnic society, social subgroups, and the family. Undoubtedly influenced by Basil Bernstein's hypothesis that forms of local social controls dictate one's linguistic code, researchers are increasingly inclined to see connections between "cognitive styles," language styles, and life styles. A mother's way of talking to her child influences the child's cast of thought, but the mother's way of talking is in turn governed by her class and ethnic heritage. If schools wish to change how students think and speak, they must take account of all the language contexts which have determined how the individual already thinks and speaks, then create a new language community that will induce what is missing. The head of any soliloquizer is peopled—long before he comes to school.

Although we customarily regard thought as private and internal, it is in many respects really very impersonal and external. Original permutations of thought may be very individualistic, but the tool of thought is an instrument socially forged from biological givens. The abstractive structures we are born with are open and flexible and may, as research in anthropology and cognitive styles shows, produce very different ab-

---

[2] *Embodiments of Mind* (Cambridge: Massachusetts Institute of Technology Press, 1965).

stractions in different groups. It is from his groups that the individual learns these *particular* ways of cognizing and verbalizing. In view of this, a pedagogy based on provoking or eliciting thought presupposes that a child is already capable of generating the required kinds of thoughts. Asking "stimulating" questions and assigning "stimulating" reading invites the student to put out but does not give him anything, as teachers of the disadvantaged know well. In order to generate some kinds of thoughts, a student must have *previously* internalized some discursive operations that will enable him to activate his native abstracting apparatus. Furthermore, it may be possible to tap inner speech too soon.

Elicitation has a place certainly at some stage of instruction, but more basic is to create the kinds of social discourse that when internalized become the kinds of cognitive instruments called for by later tasks. The failure of disadvantaged students to think and talk middle-class prose stems obviously from their not having been talked to and with in the way middle-class people talk to and with their children. But even the most advantaged child will never escape the cognitive limitations of family, class, social role, etc., unless the school provides him a kind of discursive experience to internalize that is different from what he has internalized at home. The cranium is the globe, but the globe *any* child grows up in is always too small for later purposes, especially in the chameleon civilization we know and are increasingly going to know.

Among the considerations that impel me to agree essentially with Mead, even though he seems to slight innate factors, is that his theory jibes with other important theories. When Erik Ericson relates kinds of societies to kinds of ego structures, he too is assuming that an individual is a walking model of his social world. Freud's concept of superego—the voice of conscience—is based on the notion of introjecting outside attitudes. And cognitive growth, according to Piaget, depends on expanding perspective by incorporating initially alien points of view. This "decentering" is the principal corrective to egocentrism (and ethnocentrism, geocentrism, etc.).

All this is to say that soliloquy is more than a stage device. It is really a colloquy among one's cultural, social, and familial voices. All the wickedly intricate relations of thought and speech, mind and society, heredity and environment are involved in it. As we participate in and observe the daily dramas of life, we are constantly soliloquizing at one or another level of abstraction, depending on where our attention is centered at the moment. If we are lying in bed late at night beside an inert husband, like Molly Bloom, we may dwell on memories and related feelings and reflections. We may fantasy, like Walter Mitty, in defiance of active surroundings. Or fasten hypnotically on immediate sights and sounds like Macbeth in the dagger scene. Or, like Hamlet, mix a debate on one's own fate (itself rather general) with a contemplation of man's fate (*very* general).

Whatever the abstraction level of the soliloquy, the action of soliloquizing is itself ongoing behavior, the drama of what is happening inside someone. *Speaking and writing are essentially just editing and abstracting some version of what at some moment one is thinking.* In asking a student to write something, the teacher is in effect asking him to take dictation from some soliloquy he will be having under the influence of the assignment conditions. Thus seen, the conditions of the assignment may appear in a new light. The different kinds of writing we recognize as descriptive, narrative, and reflective depend on the abstraction level of the soliloquy, which in turn depends on the soliloquizer's present attentional focus. However influenced by outside constraints, such as assignment conditions, any soliloquy is spontaneous—one does not at a given moment choose what is to come up for editing. Therefore—and this is the main point—what becomes available for someone to put on paper when he is writing has already been greatly determined by prior verbal experience. Reading is a very potent source of contents and forms which a student stores and may later utilize in soliloquy. But I am going to claim that conversational dialogue exerts the most powerful and direct influence on the content and forms of soliloquy. That is, interaction is a more important learning process than imitation, whatever the age of the learner.

DIALOGUE

Real-life conversation is primary discourse—spontaneous, ongoing, unpondered, and uncomposed. The dialogue of a play purports to be such. In a word, dialogue is *extemporized*. It is generated of the moment and moves in time, governed by setting and circumstances as well as by the wills of the speakers. Neither speaker knows what he is going to say a minute hence because that depends on what his interlocuter says in the meantime and perhaps also on what is going on around them. Face to face, each relies on nonverbal cues from voice, face, and body, as well as on the lexical meanings of the words. Feedback is fast, clearing up or aggravating misunderstanding. I call this "primary" because (1) it is the first discourse we learn; (2) it is the least abstract in the sense of least planned and ordered, however abstract individual words and statements may be; and (3) it is discourse in its most physical and behavioral form. That is, face-to-face dialogue is most localized in time and space. It blends with and depends on other physical action, both of the body and of surroundings. It relies on the interlocuters' seeing and hearing each other, on such things as ostensive communication (pointing). It is often interchangeable with other action; a kiss or a blow can replace words and vice versa. Organization by one mind is minimal, for interaction partly determines the selection and arrangement of words, ideas, and images. Continuity, topic—and even word choice and sentence structure—are governed in large measure by the social transaction.

One of the unique qualities of dialogue is that the interlocuters build on each other's sentence constructions. A conversation is verbal collaboration. Each party borrows words and phrases and structures from the other, recombines them, adds to them, and elaborates them. An exchange may consist of several kinds of operations, or rather, co-operations, such as question-answer, parry-thrust, and statement-emendation, demonstrated most powerfully in the theater by stichomythia (the rapid alternation of speakers).

Inseparable from this verbal collaboration is the accompanying cognitive collaboration. A conversation is dia-logical—a meeting and fusion of minds even if speakers disagree. Of course much conversation is not ideational but consists of ceremonial formulas, admonitions, com-

11

mands, and exhortations. But where thinking is involved at all, it is joint thinking; dual *logos* is at work. While participating in this mental duet, we are incorporating the points of view, attitudes, ideas, and modifications of ideas of our partner, even if we openly reject them.

I would like to advance an hypothesis that dialogue is the major means of developing thought and language, and to illustrate the kinds of co-operations responsible for this development.

Evidence of various sorts suggests to me that two general limitations characterize the thought and speech of younger children and of older but "disadvantaged" people—the failure to *specify* and the failure to *relate*, both of which I will subsume under the concept of *qualifying*. Specifying is an act of analysis; relating, an act of synthesis. The verbally immature or disadvantaged student needs, on the one hand, to discriminate and specify more, which would move him toward details; and, on the other, he needs to connect in, for example, temporal, causal, and contrastive ways, and to subordinate ideas to establish rank and salience, all of which would move him toward higher abstraction. Like an embryo, he needs, paradoxically, to grow simultaneously in opposite directions, toward differentiation and integration—to elaborate specialized parts within the whole, and to interrelate parts throughout the whole.

Linguistically, qualifying works out as the expansion of sentences. The undeveloped person tends to overcodify and say simply, "I saw a fight yesterday," begging a hundred questions. Or, if he does specify, to string the bits of information out into a mere list, a sequence of kernel sentences or simple clauses joined with *and* that orders and juxtaposes items in a neutral and coordinate fashion: *Yesterday I went to the playground. Two guys were fighting. I never saw them before. They were wearing black jackets and one kicked the other and there was blood . . . ,* and so on. In this latter case not only is economy sacrificed (a different but important matter) but salience and focus are missing: is the speaker's "point" or center of interest the strangeness of the fighters, the violence, or what? And lack of relatedness creates ambiguity: did the kick draw blood, or did both fighters bear blood from earlier blows?

To take specifying alone for a moment—it consists not just of finding precise nouns and verbs but of modifying the nouns with adjectives, appositives, prepositional phrases, participial phrases, and relative clauses; and similarly, of modifying the verbs with adverbs, prepositional phrases, and relative clauses indicating time, place, manner, and so on. All these elements elaborate a sentence, of course, but the information in most of these modifiers *could* be predicated in separate sentences, which, as I have said, is just what the undeveloped person tends to do first, a tendency parodied by Dick and Jane: *I see a ball. The ball is blue. It is in the grass. I saw it yesterday.* The last three sentences add to the first sentence three more facts about the ball and the speaker. This satisfies half of our requirement for qualification—specifying—but at this point all we have is enumeration of facts, a meaningless inventory. Such a sequence might be rhetorically calculated to get the gradual dawning effect of recognizing the ball, and this is indeed a fine justification for using kernels. Seldom is this the case, however, with naive speakers or basal readers (the dullness of the latter owing, precisely, to their meaningless inventories, as well as to their use of structures that trail by several years the child's development).

To fulfill the other condition of qualification—logical relation—the four kernels above might be synthesized into: "I see in the grass the blue ball I saw yesterday." Is the information the same as before? Yes, and no. We have the same four facts, but syntax has generated new information beyond any of the isolated facts, namely the main point of the whole experience, that the ball seen today and the ball seen yesterday are one and the same. The new information is of a higher order than the old information: it is about the speaker's verbal intent; it tells us what he considers salient and what is merely supportive data. Though the pronoun *it* linguistically relates the ball of today and the ball of yesterday, this intersentence connection does not suffice to synthesize the data of the four-sentence sequence, whereas the syntax of the new sentence renders the whole meaning residing in the speaker's intent. (Note that in fusing the four sentences into one I had to change the article from *a* to *the* and shift the order of *in the grass* to avoid ambiguity, the first being a semantic adjustment logically entailed by the relative clause, and the second a practical adjustment to offset one of the hazards of complexity.)

But suppose the speaker's experience was something else. Suppose when he saw the ball the day before he thought it was green: "This ball in the grass I saw yesterday is *blue*." Or the ball has changed location, from sidewalk to grass: "This blue ball I saw yesterday is now in the grass." Syntax speaks; implicitly, it conveys the more abstract, less palpable information of larger meanings. As Basil Bernstein has theorized, the undeveloped speaker assumes rather than renders his verbal intent.[1]

Except for those relatively rare cases where the accumulation of kernels best conveys our experience or idea through an inductive rhetoric that forces the reader to do the relating, it is clear, I think, that expanding kernels and other simple sentences is a necessity of mature thought and

---

[1] "Linguistic Codes, Hesitation Phenomena and Intelligence," *Language and Speech,* 5, Part I (January-March 1962), 31-46.

speech. Specifying alone remains a dubious blessing, mere addition, until the powerful calculus of syntax interrelates items to form logical wholes.

What are the resources of syntax that do this? They are several, but the chief ones are *conjoining* and *embedding*.[2] Two sentences might be connected by one of the coordinating or subordinating conjunctions, all of which except *and* are interpretive—*if, or, although, while, unless,* and so on. Or one potentially independent sentence might be embedded in another as a noun clause, relative clause, participial phrase, infinitival or gerundive nominalization, appositive, or absolute; even such noun modifiers as adjectives and prepositional phrases represent embeddings of reduced sentences. (A kernel is defined, in one way, as containing no embeddings or conjoinings.) Conjoining tends to relate items explicitly (with words that declare the relation, conjunctions). An example is: "Since they were starting another game, he decided to return later." Embedding relates implicitly (by substitution and insertion alone). An example is: "Seeing another game about to begin, he decided to return later." Although these two are the chief tools for achieving logical relation through syntax, there are others, including correlative constructions ("the more . . . the more," "not only . . . but also") and sheer juxtaposition as regards the placement of movable elements (governed by transformation rules).

I think of this critical relation between qualifying thought and elaborating sentence structures as having two levels. At the first level items are specified only; at the second, in addition to being specified, they are also related. The first level can be attained, in a single kernel, only through predicate adjectives and through certain adverbial phrases that are not embeddings; or in a sequence of kernels, through the stringing of discrete predications. Only at the second level, however, where conjoining and embedding relate these kernels can such specificity reach fruition and become true qualification. A *single kernel sentence* asserts an unqualified or barely qualified statement and thus establishes the minimum for level one. A *kernel with nonembedded modification* fulfills level one in some measure but cannot specify much without succeeding sentences. A *sequence of kernels with nonembedded modification* will in most cases still fall short of level two also, because "nonembedded modification" excludes not only noun and relative clauses but also nominalizations, participial phrases, appositives, and adjectives and prepositional

---

2 Some transformational theorists may construe subordinate conjoining as a subclass of embedding, but for my purposes here it will be clearer to treat them as different operations.

phrases modifying a noun. That is, only at level two do the full syntactic resources get put into play.

By way of doing a little qualifying myself—without, I hope, introducing too much intricacy—I should add that some sentences containing references to other sentences may remain linguistically simple while actually achieving cognitive complexity. Thus: *I like that.* (When *that* refers to a whole preceding idea). Or *In that case we should buy tickets now.* (*In that case* referring probably to a previous clause, often an *if*-clause.) Or *They disagreed nevertheless.* (*Nevertheless* acting as an intersentence connector). Since such referencing merely entails pronouns, adverbs, and adverbial phrases, it may not technically change the status of a kernel sentence, and yet it is clear that a previously predicated idea is being either incorporated into the kernel or joined to it. *In effect,* a sort of indirect embedding or conjoining has taken place, discernible at the semantic but not the linguistic level. Transformational theory has not yet dealt much with such referencing, but I would regard these sentences as a separate class of simple sentences equivalent to some more complex sentences, since this kind of referencing is just the sort of logical relating achieved by the syntax of more complex sentences. I would argue, however, that not all referencing has the same power to relate. *It,* referring to a one-word antecedent, and *however,* referring to a whole clause, stand in the same power proportion as a true kernel sentence does to a sentence containing embedding or conjoining.

The point of this analysis has been to establish a parallel between qualifying thought and elaborating sentence structures. I have treated the expansion of kernels only because the operations involved in it apply at all levels of complexity, not because the educational problem is merely one of getting beyond kernels, which most children can do in *some* measure very early. But a good linguistic education would insure that, as a student worked cognitively downward toward detail and upward toward generality, he would be helped to find, or to activate, the matching language structures. There is no virtue in complexity for its own sake but only for the sake of this matching. The only reason for encouraging a student to elaborate his sentence structures, aside from stylistic variation and rhetorical effect, is to enable him to qualify his information and communication. The less facility one has with conjoining and embedding, the more one's thought is likely to remain crude. Again, discourse does not just convey thought, it also forges it.

I think the classroom method for helping students learn to qualify thought and elaborate sentence structures should be essentially the same method by which children spontaneously learn to do these things out of school. Although direct imitation is part of the method, it is probably not the main part or the most effective; very young children will join two clauses with *because* because they have heard such sentences but may fail to establish any true causal connection. I would like to submit that the most important and successful way we learn linguistic forms is by internalizing the whole give and take of conversations. That is, the learner synthesizes what *both* A and B said, especially when he himself is one of the interlocutors, and produces in the future a new sentence that is a conjoining, embedding, or other synthesis of the two utterances. (This "future sentence" would of course not necessarily be about the same content; I am speaking of the *structural* synthesis informing the content.) Whatever the form of synthesis, he produces a more elaborate statement than was either before. This is a very different process from the learner's hearing an utterance of a certain construction one time and then at another time, in what he perceives to be a similar situation, constructing a similar sentence. This is imitation and is undoubtedly of value in acquiring language and shaping thought, but as in the causal construction, the learner is often wrong. Furthermore, although extensive reading and listening prepare for elaboration, they do not seem to activate it. Imitating one utterance, finally, is not as potent a method as synthesizing two utterances.

My proposal for teaching the use of linguistic forms through dialogue will go against the current trend to adapt scientific grammars directly to the classroom by devising exercises that resemble the linguist's own analyses. A student in such a program, for example, is asked to read a simplified theory of the grammar, then to analyze sample sentences, to think up samples of his own that are structurally like a model, and to take sentences and conjoin and embed them. I think this is misguided. The transfer of these exercises to the skills of speaking and writing is as dubious as with the old grammar exercises, whose value research has roundly disproved. Even to prove the method is possible is not to prove it is wise. Furthermore, isolated sentences lack the realistic context out of which choices of linguistic forms or sentence structures are made—that is, the context of the whole, motivated discourse. When a student needs to learn a certain structure is just when he is discoursing himself. Finally, at a given age the student knows most of the constructions that the exercises prepared for him are about; why he does not use them is apparently another issue, an issue that exercises do not deal with.

Let's look now at some of the possible operations or transactions comprising dialogue that could teach elaboration of thought and speech. One such operation may be question-and-answer. A makes a statement and B asks for more information. The answer to B's question may be a sentence or a potential sentence which if fused with A's original statement would result in a conjoining, an embedding, or some simpler expansion. At the same time, the original statement is qualified by the further information or different point of view.

A: I saw that dog again.
B: Where?
A: Down along the river.

I saw that dog again *down along the river.*

(Verb modification with a locative phrase.)

A: I saw that dog again.
B: Which one?
A: That shaggy one we found in the barn yesterday.

I saw that *shaggy* dog again *that we found in the barn yesterday.*

(Embedding—adjective and relative clause.)

A: The bill will never pass.
B: Why not?
A: It's too close to elections.

The bill will never pass *because it's too close to elections.*

(Subordinate conjoining—causal.)

A: The bill will never pass.
B: Never?
A: Well, I mean it can't until after elections.

The bill can't pass *until after elections.*

(Subordinate conjoining—temporal.)

A: I just talked with Mr. Anaheim.
B: Who's he?
A: The assistant director of the program.

I just talked with Mr. Anaheim, *the assistant director of the program.*

(Embedding—appositive.)

In the following operation B directly embeds A's utterance:

A: He won't talk to them.
B: Whether he talks to them or not makes no difference.

(Embedding—noun clause.)

A: Who's going to help him get out of that mess?
B: His getting out of that mess is no business of ours.

(Embedding—gerundive nominalization.)

B may incorporate or annex the main idea of A's utterance by referring to it, but may not directly embed the utterance. Needing to refer and not wishing to repeat, B finds a linguistic structure accommodating both A's idea and his own overlying idea.

A: Who's going to help him get out of that mess?
B: That's not our business.
    or
    Regardless of his mess, we have to go ahead.

A: I think the price is too high for them.
B: They'll pay despite the price (whatever the price) (nevertheless).

Another operation consists simply of appending a qualifying clause to the original statement:

A: He'll make it, don't worry.   He'll make it *if he finds the key*
B: If he finds the key in time.   *in time.*

(Subordinate conjoining—conditional.)

A: These angles will always be   These angles will always be equal
    equal, then.   *so long as these lines are parallel.*
B: So long as these lines are
    parallel.

(Correlative conjoining.)

Perhaps the most important operation occurs when B adds to A's statement another fact, point of view, or argument that (he implies) A should allow for. The conjunctive or embedding relation between the two statements is only implied in the conversation but would be supplied by A in a future discourse:

A: Government ownership of rail-   Although government ownership
    roads would not work in the   of railroads has worked in En-
    U. S.   gland and France, it would not
B: It has worked in England and   work in the U. S.
    France.

(Subordinate conjoining—concessive.)

or

The fact that government ownership of railroads has worked in
England and France does not
mean it will work in the U. S.
(Embedding—noun clause.)

A: Miss Leary scowls all the time   Miss Leary scowls all the time,
    and makes you stand outside   makes you stand outside the door,
    the door.   and gives the lowest grades in the
B: I've heard that she gives the   whole school.
    lowest grades in the whole
    school.

(Coordinate conjoining—additive.)

or

Miss Leary not only scowls all the
time and makes you stand outside
the door, she also gives the lowest
grades in school.
(Correlative conjoining.)

A: King Alfred voluntarily abdi-   Already stripped of his power by
    cated.   the assembly, King Alfred volun-
B: But that was after the assembly   tarily abdicated.
    had already stripped him of
    his power.

(Embedding—participial phrase.)

These examples are crude compared to the dynamics of continuous dialogue, where this process of questioning, appending, and amending may continue across many utterances, and sometimes with A further elaborating B's contributions. Also, the reader will have to extrapolate from these examples to more complicated dialogues involving multiple speakers.

The qualifying of thought and elaborating of sentence structures develop together. Outside the classroom this development through vocal exchange occurs all the time, but in the classroom it can be furthered deliberately by creating kinds of dialogue in which questioning, collaborating, qualifying, and calling for qualification, are habitual give-and-take operations. Adjustive feedback by no means requires an adult always, but an adult may be necessary to establish the necessary characteristics of the conversation. If interlocutors do not really engage with each other, pick up cues, and respond directly, or if they merely listen out the other and wait for their turn to speak, nothing very educational will happen.

I am asking the reader to associate dialogue with dialectic. The internal conversation we call thinking recapitulates previous utterances *as amended and expatiated on.* The social actions underlying vocal exchange have counterparts in the forms of language. Dialogical structures and linguistic structures can be translated into each other. Thus what *can* seem like dead, academic matters in a classroom are drama-tizable.

This is easiest to see with conjoining, because conjunctions are explicit. Additives represent agreement; adversatives, contradiction; concessives, provisos, and conditionals, a degree of acceptance and a degree of resistance. (More naive students tend toward additive and adversative operations only—the full agreement of *and* or full disagreement of *but*—and need to have other possibilities demonstrated for them.) Constructions of time, place, and manner are born of when, where, and how questions motivated by the listener's desire to get more information from his speaker. The true *because* is born of *why.* The creation of relative clauses and the insertion of interpretive "signal words" like *however, moreover,* and *therefore* stem from a felt need to relate statements for the benefit of the listener. The way the speaker becomes aware of this need is through questions of clarification or other feedback indicating that the listener does not understand the relations among items or statements in the utterance.

Although a student might come to use connectors, expand modifiers, subordinate clauses, and embed sentences just by sheer imprinting—

stylistic imitation—I think it is safe to say that such learning would never go far or deep without the functional need for qualification and elaboration arising in dialogue. This is why I do not think exercises with dummy sentences, no matter how superior the grammar, will teach students how to use various linguistic constructions appropriately and habitually. The expatiation process of dialogue adjusts a speaker's verbal and cognitive instruments at just the moment when he cares most and in just the way that he, individually, needs this adjustment.

MONOLOGUE

The first movement away from dialogue is monologue, by which I mean the sustained, connected speech of the sort the term designates in the theater. It is the opposite of stichomythia, which represents dramatic crest, the high point of fast verbal interaction when interlocutors shoot single sentences or half sentences at each other in rapid alternation. Notoriously, monologue risks breaking a play, because the longer one speaker holds forth, the more the content of his speech overshadows his interaction with other players. Most television scenarists make it a point of never letting a character utter more than two or three sentences at a time.

Whatever prompts a monologuist to talk so long carries with it some continuity or organizing principle that is likely to take the audience out of the present. If the monologue is a report of what happened, it goes into the past; if a generality about what happens, it goes into a timeless realm. Besides chronological and logical continuities, a third possibility exists—a sequence ordered by some psychologic—but such a monologue approaches soliloquy again and, indeed, is usually played by the actor with a certain self-absorption as a kind of musing. In all cases, monologue tends to carry us away from the existential circumstances of its utterance and to lessen interaction with a listener, but the psychological sequence remains more dramatic than the chronological or logical because, like a soliloquy, it has the present dynamic of moment-to-moment inner movement. The great success of Jerry's monologues in *The Zoo Story* is due to the fact that his stories and generalizations are themselves strongly enchained by a psychologic stemming from his intention to break Peter open and reach him, to find out if continuing to live is worth it.

Monologue is the bridge from drama to other forms of discourse. It is the beginning of a speech less moored to circumstance and audience, that floats more freely in time and space. It moves closer to organization and composition, because *some single mind is developing a subject*. It is the external pathway to writing. And yet, ultimately, every monologue has some dialogue for its context, from which it issues. This is true whether the monologue is an anecdote in a back porch gossip session, the Greek messenger's report of Hippolytus' death, or a novel. Lest the third example seem out of order, let me suggest that any written composition may be usefully deemed a monologue, since it is uttered entirely by one person, and that the dialogue from which it issues is simply more extended over time and space. The solo work we call a novel is part of a slow-moving, long-range dialogue-at-a-distance between the novelist and his society. Feedback comes in the form of public response, sales, reviews, and critical articles.

Among monologues, then, the critical distinction is between the face-to-face vocalizations, which are extemporaneous and very sensitive to audience presence and to circumstances of utterance, and written monologues, which are planned and composed in relative detachment from audience and circumstances. Further, among written monologues themselves there are degrees of composedness and detachment: consider a scale going from kinds of private, occasional writing such as letters, memos, and diaries to duplicated and published writing directed at an increasingly widespread audience.

If the teacher imagines a continuum going from the one extreme of stichomythia to the other extreme of the polished solo publication, he has then an instrument of pedagogical value. For the gradations of the continuum are steps in a natural evolution from dialogue to written composition. A cumulative learning sequence can be based on these gradations that will lead the student from conversation to vocal monologue to casual writing to formal writing. (As I have indicated, a simultaneous development toward writing derives from soliloquy by an internal route.) But the first step toward writing is made when a speaker takes over a conversation and sustains some subject alone. He has started to create a solo discourse that while intended to communicate to others is less collaborative, less prompted, and less corrected by feedback than dialogue. He bears more of the responsibility for effective communication. He has moved away from drama toward narrative, exposition, and theory—the domains of writing. He has started to enchain his utterances according to some logic. The cues for his next line are not what his interlocutor said but what he himself just said. Like a jazz solo, a monologue grows by self-stimulation.

When ongoing social behavior no longer structures the discourse, some internal behavior, some logic, takes over and determines the order and arrangement of utterances. Even such one-way action as admonition, exhortation, and command cannot be sustained unless some logic is resorted to and some "argument" set in motion. To abandon the transaction of dialogue for the transmission of monologue is to drop interrogative and imperative modes and to work solely in the declarative mode.

The more independent the monologue is from listen and situation, the more it becomes statement.

What enchains the consecutive declarations of the monologuist is some fusion of logical connections and rhetorical ploys. For example, chronological order might be disarranged to put an arresting event first, or the conclusion of a syllogistic argument might be placed either first or last depending on the effect desired. What is characteristic of monologue, however, and not of dialogue is the unfolding of a subject according to the logic and rhetoric of one mind. I can only suggest here what is the subject of another essay—the possible types of monological sequences. They may be arrayed in an abstractive hierarchy ranging from the "then ... then" of chronology to the "if ... then" of formal argument.

In another way monologue evolves from dialogue. This evolution concerns the embedding of one kind of discourse within another. The brief utterances of a dialogue may be of all sorts—a bit of description, a one- or two-sentence story, a general proposition, or an if-then syllogism. Each such utterance is a miniature monologue. The form of predication is the seed of a whole monological structure. A past tense verb, say, with modifiers of time and place foreshadows the full story predicated likewise in narrative form but allotting several sentences to one action and perhaps whole paragraphs or even longer sections to establishing time and place. The difference of course is, again, elaboration. Similarly, the one-sentence proposition or syllogism is the seed of an utterance that, if extended and elaborated, resembles what we call an exposition or argumentation. A sizable slice of conversation usually contains, embedded in it here and there, fragments of all these modes of discourse which can be developed into monologues and thence into compositions. In fact, a child can, in brief utterances, handle any of these modes, for he has the linguistic structures necessary to describe, narrate, frame a generality, and (unless badly disadvantaged) employ the if-then construction. What, precisely, he does not characteristically do is extend and elaborate these utterances beyond a sentence or two (clearly he does so sooner with description and narration)—that is, order utterances into a continuity that translates the small-unit structure of the sentence into the large-unit structure of a monologue.

A good English teacher would help the student, of whatever age, to take wing and extend one of these embodied bits of narrative or exposition. A younger student would be encouraged to sally forth from amidst a dialogue. The older student might within one class period traverse on a small scale the whole continuum of dialogue → vocal monologue → written monologue that I mentioned before as a curriculum sequence.[1] That is, he converses in a small group, extends one of his utterances before the entire class, then takes the monologue to paper and finishes it there, thus moving through a short version of the general learning progression. Because they are both mono-logical, whatever the degree of improvisation or composition, any vocal holding forth contains the same possibilities for various kinds of continuity as any written holding forth.

To ask a student to write is to ask him to make all the adjustments between dialogue and monologue that I have been describing. I am saying that a curriculum should afford the student a rich experience in not only the right kinds of conversation but also in the variety of vocal and written monologues that bridge into full-fledged public composition. The most critical adjustment one makes is to relinquish collaborative discourse, with its reciprocal prompting and cognitive co-operation, and to go it alone. The first going it alone can be simply an extended utterance within a conversation. A very important issue of psychological independence is involved. Failing to achieve this independence is a major reason why so many students—even adolescents—who can converse for hours claim they have "nothing to say" when asked to write.

Also, forsaking the interrogative and imperative modes for declaration eliminates a lot of discourse that a child is most familiar with. Add to this the well-known fact that an enormous amount of conversation is social communion, establishing and maintaining solidarity, and has little to do with developing a subject, which in fact is sometimes a pretty indifferent matter. Add further that having to develop a real subject, alone, means employing one or more of the monological orders of statement. Where does the student find such things? Only in himself of course. And how do they get there? They get there through internalization of previous dialogues. . . .

Monologue derives from past dialogue via the internal route of soliloquy, and derives from present dialogue by soloing out of ensembles. When anyone verbalizes solo fashion, whether silently to himself, aloud to another, or on paper to the world, he must draw on discourse he has heard, had, and read. A student can give to the world only some permutations of what he got from the world. Lest this seem to slight the powers of the individual, let me add, perhaps paradoxically, that the more speech of other people one takes in, the more original will be his permutations and the freer will he be of any limited set of voices. Liberation is a matter of hearing out the world.

---

[1] For this suggestion I am indebted to Douglas Barnes of the University of Leeds.

In summary, drama is the matrix of discourse. As information, it is the inner speech of the observer at the moment of coding raw phenomena. The corresponding educational activity is recording. As communication, it is the social speech of the participant at the moment of vocalizing face to face. The corresponding educational activity is oral extemporizing. Soliloquy is intrapersonal dialogue, which is verbal thought. Conversation is interpersonal dialogue, which is vocal speech. These two activities feed each other: when we communicate we internalize conversation that will influence how we code information in soliloquy; how we inform ourselves in soliloquy will influence what we communicate in conversation.

TEACHING METHODS

Let me turn now to the actual teaching methods that relate to these considerations of drama. Most of these methods have been tried at the elementary or secondary level in some public and private schools. The appropriate classroom activities may be roughly divided into active discoursing by the student—conversing and writing—and the receptive occupations such as listening, reading, and beholding. But it is in the nature of dramatic methods that this division should not hold well, for what is output for one student is often input for another. In fact, all of these activities would be woven in and out of each other.

Because it is primary, I will begin with face-to-face vocalization, which breaks down into four activities—dramatic improvisation, discussion, play performing, and monologuing. These are closely related and one can grow out of others.

Dramatic Improvisation

An improvisation is spur-of-the-moment invention of action. But this invention is done within some framework of givens or stipulations. Indeed, younger children seem to need more givens, whereas experienced improvisers can start with a bare suggestion or minimal situation. The givens may at first be props, puppets, or bits of costume that stipulate place (grocery store), personage (Smoky Bear), or role (king). Later, these stipulations may be made abstractly: A is a parent, B a child, and B is making an excuse of some kind—an assignment of situation and relationship—or, very abstractly, A wants B to stay and C wants him to go—an assignment of a certain triadic dynamic.

By contrast with the extreme openness of the last situation, where the actors have to supply personalities, relationships, and circumstances, a very restricted form of improvisation is the enacting of stories the students have read or been told. Since, as I have said, drama elaborates narrative, what happens in this case is that the actors fill in the details of body movement and dialogue. Though it may be helpful to distinguish between *invention* and *enactment,* these two forms are only relative since the actors are always working within the constraints of some set of givens. In general, younger and less experienced children want to do

26

roles and stories already familiar and only gradually abandon stereotypes and conventions for more original creation.

The method shifts somewhat with the age and dramatic experience of the students, but in general everybody is participating simultaneously without an audience—either in several small groups or as one class group. The story or situation to be improvised is usually discussed first. It may be a familiar domestic situation, a bit of history or social studies material, or a piece of literature. Different groups might work on the same "scene" or consecutive "scenes." Roles are rotated (no type casting) and different versions done until the potentialities of the situation have been well explored, or, of the story, well elaborated and extended. If a group wants to repeat its improvisation before the rest of the class, fine, but the goal is not performance, and the teacher does not push toward it. At a very advanced stage, however, the class may become a kind of drama workshop in which the sub-groups expect to improvise before the others so that everything can be discussed—the dynamics, the content, the roles and styles, the acting.

In fact, a powerful side effect of improvisation is the dialogue *about* the improvisation generated before, during, and after. Such conversation concerns both the task itself and ideas embodied in the material. That is, the whole class, or the subgroups, discuss the choices of material, differences in various versions of it, consequent differences in interpretations, and hence ideas, perceptions, and values. Task-oriented or problem-centered talk turns naturally onto psychological, moral, and literary issues. Or conversely, a discussion taking off from a different point, such as direct considerations of psychological and moral issues or difficulties with a piece of literature, can turn toward improvisations for exemplification and clarification. Improvisation should be thought of as a learning process that can be exploited for many discursive purposes.

One of these is specifically literary. Before a child can enjoy drama in script form—play reading—he can do so by creating the imitative actions of which scripts are a blueprint. Later, his power to bring a script alive in his mind is constantly recharged by his continued experience in inventing dramas. For narrative, improvisation renders a special service: it translates *what happened* back to *what is happening*. For younger children this brings back to present actuality—alive—the abstraction of a story they read silently on the page or had read aloud to them. For older students, converting narrative to drama demonstrates the relationship of the two: plays specify what narrative summarizes, and narrative, unlike drama, is told by someone addressing us.

Furthermore, many fairy tales, legends, myths, and histories are extremely condensed and often told very impersonally. They lack physical detail, dialogue, and the personal points of view of either the characters or the narrator—all things that make a story more interesting and more like familiar fiction. Improvisation allows students to imagine and fill in these physical details and dialogue and, through invented soliloquies, also the thoughts and feelings of the characters. Difficulties of text, too, can yield to the process of being "cast in other terms," the existential terms of drama. And, finally, improvisation can be used as an entrée into a literary work soon to be read: the teacher abstracts key situations —say, Cassius' efforts to persuade Brutus to join the conspiracy—and assigns this as a situation to improvise before students read the work, so that when they do read it they already have an understanding of what is happening and of how differently the characters *might* have behaved. This kind of prelude also involves students more with the text.

There are several, more fundamental purposes of dramatic improvisation. Begun at an early uninhibited age, extemporizing of this sort can head off later self-consciousness, make verbalization easy and natural, increase presence of mind, and develop inventiveness. But this is only a basic discursive facility, a loosening of tongue and limbering of wit. More specific goals are to foster the ability to (1) listen closely and react directly to an interlocutor, (2) devise *ad hoc* rhetorical ploys for getting certain effects and results, (3) simulate the language, style, voice, and manner of someone of a certain type or role, (4) shift roles, attitudes, and points of view—stand in others' shoes, (5) feel from the inside the dynamics that make up a theatrical scene, and (6) act out and express real feelings in a situation made safe by the pretense that "I am being someone else."

Discussion

Discussion is another kind of oral improvisation but one especially intended to exploit the inherent relation between dialogue and dialectic. It is a dramatic method of developing intellectual powers. The main purpose is to promote the social art of conversing, the intellectual art of qualifying, and the linguistic art of elaborating. The right kind of dialogue will teach so-called exposition and argumentation better than years of premature belaboring on paper. The characteristics, listed above, that improvisation is designed to develop should transfer readily to discussion because the context is the same—face-to-face vocalization—and so is the process—feeding back and expatiating.

Differences are of degree: in discussion, body movement is minimized and the givens—topics—are simply stipulated so abstractly (by comparison) that concrete "scenes" become examples to allude to rather than to act out (although at any point in a discussion a group might resort to improvisation). And whereas improvisations *embody* ideas and issues, discussions deal with them explicitly and only verbally. It is possible, however, to shade gradually between improvisation and discussion. If the participants of a drama begin to talk directly about the issues their acts involve, or to invoke concepts, as in talky plays, then the drama shifts toward discussion, physical action being minimized and the dialogue centering on a "topic." In fact, a transitional stage between the two could be created by asking students to discuss a topic while assuming a certain social role or personality other than their own, perhaps that of a character in a book.

The size of discussion groups should be small, a group of no more than six taken aside by the teacher while the rest of the class is doing something else. Sometimes several such groups might be discussing at the same time, if they have had enough experience and if space permits. Occasionally, discussions by the whole class or half of it are worthwhile, especially when preparing to launch subgroups into separate work on a project or when bringing them back together to exchange results and combine experiences. In general, large groups are poor for *learning* to discuss and can only reap the benefits of this learning.

What the group discusses may be a book they have read in common, a student paper, an improvisation or performance by some of its members, an abstract topic of general interest, or many other things. I am concerned here with *how* they talk, with honing a fine cognitive tool out of extemporaneous conversation. The teacher's special talent, for which he must be trained, is to play a dialogue by ear and exploit the unforeseen twists and turns of it to explore all those things that textbooks ineffectually try to present to students in an exposition. Discussion of student and professional writing, for example, will naturally raise issues of what we call rhetoric, style, logic, semantics, grammar, literary form, and composition. What a student of language needs is not external facts but more insight about what he and his peers are doing verbally and what they could be doing. The teacher's knowledge of linguistics, semantics, or literary form, say, must influence the student. But the best method of influence is dramatic, not expository. The teacher's art is to open up the whole range of external, social operations that will lead to internal, cognitive operations. He does this by getting students to feed back to each other. Once they are independent of him, he may inject more of his experience into the conversation; but because such monologues should arise directly from their dialogue, the monologues can't be planned. The group should collaboratively forge serviceable abstractions and thus enable each member to do so alone.

The composition of groups—and hence of classes—should be as various as possible. Individuals would be in one group formed for one purpose and in another formed for another purpose. But for the sake of a rich multiplicity of dialects, vocabulary, styles, ideas, and points of view, the class should be heterogeneously sectioned from a diverse student population. It should constitute the most powerful multilingual assembly that can be brought together. This means mixing levels of ability and achievement, mixing sexes, mixing races, and mixing socioeconomic classes. At times even ages should be temporarily mixed, and outside adults should come in and join discussions. Certainly the internalization process is severely curtailed if urban and suburban children, advantaged and disadvantaged, do not talk together. Not only will they have to "speak each other's language" in the future, for social and political reasons, but the language of each needs something from the other. Disadvantaged urban children can learn standard English only by speaking with people who use it. But, which is more important, they need to learn new *uses* of language—how to think by means of it, solve problems with it, influence others, and bring about action. Advantaged children living in *sub*urban ghettos will not be sacrificed by mixing. They need to relearn constantly the emotive and communal uses of language that middle-class upbringing tends to destroy. And their language needs the mythic and metaphoric qualities of lower-class speech. But all this means breaking the socioeconomic gerrymandering of large cities and restructuring school districts along metropolitan rather than municipal lines. If the educational ideal is to expand to the fullest the verbal and cognitive repertory of students, then the biggest single obstacle is in-grouping of all sorts, from familial to cultural.

Group discussion is a fundamental activity that should be a staple learning process from kindergarten through college. It is an activity to be learned both for its own sake and for the sake of learning other things by means of it. It is a major source of that discourse which the student will transform internally into thought. To do and be these things, it must become a highly wrought tool considerably different from what generally passes in schools today for "class discussion." To be clear about "right kind of dialogue," let me contrast current practices with some other models.

First of all, with rare exceptions most "class discussions" are actually serial dialogues between teacher and student A, then student B, etc. The model for this kind of exchange is the furniture arrangement—a block of little desks all facing the teacher's desk, which is isolated in front. The assumption seems to be that students can learn only from the teacher. There are several faults in the assumption and in that kind of conversation. For one thing, the proper development of thought requires operations other than question and answer—those corresponding, for example, to the additive, adversative, conditional, and concessive constructions of language. And usually the student is on one end only of the operation, the answer end. Think too of the multiplicity of attitudes represented by any mixed class of twenty or thirty students—the range of points of view and emendations going to waste. These do not have to be emitted by a teacher, and indeed often they could not be. Furthermore, emendation by the authority figure frequently elicits resistance because the student may associate it with "big people always trying to tell you what to do—even what to think."

The teacher should promote honest student-to-student conversation. His job is to help students learn from each other. If each student has to get clearance from the teacher to speak, interaction among students has little chance to take place. The raising of hands should be abolished but a ground rule of not interrupting held to. Small children will perhaps want to talk at once, and the beginning might be difficult, but if we are to convert "collective monologues"—simultaneous egocentric speeches—into real dialogue, the pupils must learn to listen and to respond to external as well as internal stimuli. Most of the furious flagging of hands and clamorous talking at once in traditional classes is actually provoked by the teacher, who usually has asked a question to which he knows the answer. The children, in competitively bidding for the teacher's approval, place no value on what other children say. The teacher must shed this parental role as dispenser of rewards and punishments and quit exploiting sibling rivalry to get right answers. It is ridiculously naive to construe as learning fervor the efforts of children to find psychic security.

Many teachers equate discussion with head-on contention. A "hot debate" is considered ideal even if it is a deadening clash of fixed ideas or a feverish struggle of egos. Cognitive development requires much more than sheer contention, which represents only the adversative operation and which frequently just solidifies everyone's ideas. Good discussion is chiefly qualifying statements, looking for what one *can* accept in an assertion and determining what one *cannot* accept. There is practically no statement one can think of that does not have some truth potential if properly qualified. The art is to stipulate the exact conditions under which some proposition *is* true, starting perhaps with the time, place, people, and circumstances to which it actually applies; then to quantify it *(all, some);* then to amend it with conditional, concessive, and proviso clauses. Vapid conclusions such as "it all depends on the individual" and "it's just a matter of semantics" are no substitute for trying to tailor a linguistic utterance to fit the reality one is talking about.

Good discussion also includes the "rules of evidence." Besides qualification, the only process that makes the difference between sound argumentation and a boring reiteration of opinions is invoking some material or logical reasons for accepting a statement. Evidence may be a narrative or anecdote, a syllogism, or a citation of some authoritative judgment or finding. The presence or absence of evidence, the nature of it, and the validity of it should become issues in the small groups.

Although formal debate as practiced by clubs and diplomats may help teach the presenting of evidence, I'm afraid I must take a strong stand against this kind of discourse in education. When someone is assigned in advance a position to champion, come hell or high water, the main point quickly becomes contention, not the search for truth. Formal debate is a game of one-upmanship, an unproductive duel of personalities. The goal is to overwhelm the opposition, not to enlarge one's mind. In my experience, debating societies always include in their membership the most dogmatic students in a school, who are drawn to such an activity because it offers an easy identity and an outlet for their talents of rationalization. It is true that part of debating is to learn to argue either side and to foresee the opponent's arguments, but this incorporation of the other's point of view is much better accomplished when one is not obliged by a prior investment to defend against that other point of view. I have several other objections to formal debating: both the dualistic format and the yes-or-no wording of topics cast issues in a crude either-or way that militates against relativistic thinking; the two parties often do not talk to the same point because their speeches are prepared; there is no feedback or interaction except in the rebuttal; and the speakers are in effect learning to ignore and talk past each other, an all too common trait of everyday conversation and diplomacy.

I am of course not trying to kill controversy. People do have and will maintain points of view in which, for one reason or another, they have an investment. What needs to be fostered, partly through controversy, is multiplicity of ideas, fertility, choice. The principle I am invoking is the old concept of the open market of ideas. A two-valued, prestructured, precommitted discourse does not live up to this principle. As an adversary game like chess or tennis, debate is fine, but it should not be a model for learning dialogue, which must include more than the adversative. Taking a position is not difficult and hardly needs to be taught; it comes to us readily with our natural egocentrism and ethnocentrism. What takes learning is the sense of alternative possibilities and the reasons for choosing one over another. Real truth seeking has always been a collaboration of receptive minds; it requires a willingness *to be influenced*, reciprocity, which is a strength not a weakness. It is the lack of this honest ingredient that leads to so many international deadlocks: one wants to manipulate the other fellow and remain unchanged oneself. This sort of "debate" is mere propaganda. Certainly the social needs of the future will exact a superior kind of dialogue than we have taught and learned in the past. The threat that collaborative conversation poses to the ego is loss of identity, but it is patent that identity can and must be based on something more enduring than a certain ideological stance.

To characterize the kind of group operation I have in mind, I need to compare it to two rather well-known models. One is the kind of workshop long employed for apprentice actors, dancers, and craftsmen. The master sets the tasks (initially anyway), the apprentices present their productions to the group, and they all explore together the issues entailed by the tasks. The content is the students' productions and some brought in from the outside. The teacher's role is the natural one he has by virtue of being more experienced in the craft; he talks freely at times like any other member but does not feel obliged to preschedule what is to be talked about (his tasks may do this in a general way) or to center discussion around himself. He fosters cross-education among the students, and they focus on the tasks, not the teacher. Each learns both from garnering reactions to his own work and from reacting in turn to the work of others. All become highly involved in what the others are doing, not only because they are engaged in the same tasks but, more importantly, because they are a social unit that is allowed to be precisely that.

The other model is the "awareness group," one offshoot of the manifold thing called group dynamics. Whereas group therapy may release psychic forces that only a psychiatrist should be expected to manage, other kinds of dynamics have been successfully used in many practical groups, such as management training, to induce awareness in individuals of what roles they automatically take in a group, how others are reacting to them, how they are attempting to handle certain social relations, and what motives lie behind their own responses to others' behavior. Such things govern the kinds of co-operations that can take place. In other words, instead of ignoring the underlying drama of what is happening among the communicants and steamrolling ahead to get on with the "business," the "business" is construed as including both the objective task and the drama engendered in working on that task. The investments that corporations, institutions, and the armed services have made in such training attest to its practicality. Of course, it is up to classroom experimentation to establish the kind and degree of insight appropriate for different ages, but some steady source of insight is indispensable. Miscommunication, poor collaboration, and distortion of the task will occur if the human relations of the class are ignored or dealt with summarily as though they were a mere nuisance.

Furthermore, the awareness group is practical for language teaching in another way: a class is, like any constituted group, a miniature communication system; if the members pay attention to its workings, they can learn more about what makes and breaks communication than any book on the subject can possibly get across. The connection with the theater is closer than one might suspect. A playwright presents a model of our behavior—especially verbal behavior—so contrived as to reveal what is *really* happening, to give insights about motive, relationship, and interaction. What makes these insights so difficult to achieve in the heat of real life is our inability to act and see simultaneously. Witnessing a play, we have an opportunity to *see*. But if the ground rules of a group permit halting the action to review it a moment, and deflecting attention from content to people, then individuals can overcome participation-blindness and attain some of the insights afforded in the theater. A duality defines such a group, then—between involvement and detachment, between the communication and the metacommunication, the exposition and the drama.

The teacher's role in small group discussions shifts as students mature and acquire conversing experience.[1] In the beginning, it is to guide the *process* without contributing to the *substance* of the conversation; later when students can run the process themselves and can express themselves independently of the teacher's viewpoint, the teacher may either leave them to themselves or participate on an equal footing and say what he really thinks. Guiding the process consists of light organizing and prompting: the teacher helps the group settle on a topic they understand in the same way; calls attention to marked irrelevance, definitional misunderstanding, and personal relations thwarting the talk; occasionally draws in shyer members; and suggests other strategies when a given line of attack on a topic has proven fruitless. With older students, the teacher may continue to induce awareness of structural and interpersonal

[1] For some clarification of this role I have benefited from reading Babette Whipple, *The Grouptalk*, Occasional Paper #10 (Watertown, Mass.: Educational Services Inc., January 1967). Though developed in a social studies program, her method is quite relevant to any course of verbal and cognitive learning.

difficulties while at the same time demonstrating by example the best ways of commenting and questioning substantively. Experience in dramatic improvisation, also, should help develop desirable characteristics of discussion such as attending closely, participating freely, responding directly, and interplaying rhetorically.

Thoroughly experienced and confident in unwitnessed discussion, the small group might converse before the rest of the class and thus become a panel, in the same way unwitnessed improvisations eventually become performances. Such a panel remains spontaneous and undivided into camps or teams. The witnessing portion of the class is provided with a detached relationship to the communicants and their ideas; this should make for calmer assessment of the ideas presented and greater awareness of dynamics in the large group. When the panel is over, the spectators can discuss both the dialectic and the drama of the panelists. Also, representatives from each small group may constitute a panel charged with discussing further what each group has discussed. This cross-fertilizes ideas from different groups.

Performing Scripts

Performing planned plays, written by either professionals or students, is a natural concomitant of improvising. Improvisation should make acting performances better, but performance creates new problems, such as memorizing the script and blocking the action, that are peculiar to planned drama. Although rehearsals take more time, they are more worthwhile than sight readings, which are rendered rather ineffectual by stumbling reading and encumbrance with the script. Short one-acters written by students would often serve well, and subsequent discussion of the performance could relate acting to writing. Putting on professional plays makes for more effective and pleasurable literary study than reading them, at least until students have had enough experience participating and witnessing to be able to bring the script to life in their minds. Performing a play offers the same opportunities as improvisation to play different roles, to attitudinize, and to develop fluency, but it may be an easier way for some students because the words and deeds are already given. Last, in memorizing and speaking lines from a script, a student is internalizing the language, style, thought, and point of view of a voice and personality probably different from his own.

I will not speak at length about play performing because it is commonly done in schools. But I will call attention to mistaken views of it or neglected aspects.

First, the point of performing is the learning experience it provides, not showing off to parents and the public. Too often performance is limited to a rare big production for presentation to outsiders and is relegated to extracurricular activities. I think there should be much more in-class performing of small pieces—short student scripts and scenes from professional plays. Small groups could exchange scripts, or choose scenes, discuss them, and work up a production, each group performing in turn.

Second, play performance should be interwoven with improvisation and script writing, not just come as climax or dessert to the reading of a play. Improvisations on a similar situation may be necessary to insure comprehension of a scene or involvement with it. And acting and writing can illuminate each other.

Third, besides student and professional play scripts, short stories and many poems are also candidates for performance. With short stories, the *narrator* as well as the characters is assigned an actor. Thus, in addition to speaking the dialogue and enacting the movement, the performers also give stage voice to the speaker of the story. This method, which has been beautifully worked out in a technique called Chamber Theater,[2] permits the dramatizing of different narrator-character relationships and hence of fictional point of view. As for poems, many are soliloquy, dramatic monologue, or dialogue and can be performed as they are; many more are narratives that can be performed in the Chamber Theater technique used for fiction.

Monologuing

The last of the vocal activities is monologuing. While becoming fluent in the give and take of conversation, a student should be induced to detach himself from the group and to talk alone. Giving a prepared speech is an act of composition followed by a reading; delivery is not what I have in mind here, but rather a kind of spontaneous monologue that would prepare for composition. As a gradual weaning, I suggest letting individuals take over the conversation for longer and longer durations, to supply anecdotes or special knowledge they may have about some aspect of a subject that is before the group. If the discussion is on transportation, the child of a bus driver might be asked to relay things his father has told him. Reading aloud one's written composition is also an easy habituation to monologuing. Next, individuals would be asked to

---

[2] Carolyn Fitchett, "An English Unit. Chamber Theater Technique," Unpublished but copyrighted 1966 by the Program for Pre-College Centers, a division of Educational Services Inc. The technique was introduced by Professor Robert S. Breen of Northwestern University and further developed by Miss Fitchett.

summarize a panel or group discussion, a more difficult organizing task than telling a narrative. With more meaningful ground rules, the show-and-tell sessions could also serve to develop powers of monologue. That is, a student who has brought something to class is somewhat in the expert's position and therefore a logical monologuist, but without involved questions from his peers he may just mutter a few words and the matter will end with "How nice." There is no reason for show-and-tell not to continue into the later years. As strong hobbies and competencies grow, older children will have a lot more to say about the things they bring in—how they work, the history, procedures, etc.—things that provide a natural outline of an extended utterance but that don't need to be prepared. It is better to let the student present his information spontaneously and for him to learn, through questions and other feedback, what might have been a better way to say what he had to say. Such a monologue could serve as the base for a written piece later.

Recording

I think it is clear how drama, narrative, exposition, and argumentation can be learned in some measure without writing a word, through oral improvisation. The oral activities are basic but not in the sense of being limited to elementary school alone; I think they should be interwoven with writing throughout secondary school as well. The activities I am going to take up now would constitute some of the child's first writing but would also recur as later assignments too. In rough summary these activities are two—eyewitness recording and playwriting. Of course, considered as productions by one individual, both are monological; that is, the student must enchain the utterances by himself. But both recording and invented dialogue are based on the same enchainment— time order of occurrence, the simplest of all. "Then . . . then." Then I see this. Then he says this. The difference is that an eyewitness has fewer decisions to make about what to put down than a playwright, because the events are given and not invented.

For recording, the student is placed in an observer relation to some phenomena and asked to dictate or write down what he registers with his senses at a particular time and place. The result is a kind of perceptual soliloquy, either in the form of telegraphic notations or of more leisurely sentences. The key tense is the progressive present; the student is verbalizing *as* he registers, and that is the definition of recording. The records thus produced are aimed at no other audience than himself and are not to be judged as communications, which they do not purport to be.

The three-fold purpose is to develop powers of observation, produce material that can subsequently be rewritten for an outside audience, and learn to abstract sensations into words. Perceptual abstraction is the first stage of symbolizing experience and a necessary condition for thinking and writing. Many so-called *writing* faults, such as lack of detail, lack of example, indiscrimination, and inaccuracy are traceable to poor observation. Starting with raw sensory data well nigh eliminates stale imitation and thus increases originality. Also, in order to become aware of how he processes information all the time, the student needs to examine *all* phases of his abstracting. Selected and told from a later point of view, a record becomes a narrative of either a personal or scientific sort. Or the notations can become the stage directions and action of a play. A sound record among people may produce an actual dialogue. In other words, a recording may be used almost as is, or it may be abstracted to further levels for different purposes and audiences. The student learns that material for writing is all around him at any given moment. The problem of prewriting—finding subjects and treating them in stages that lead to a finished product—can be solved, I believe, by spontaneous recording, which is another kind of improvisation.

The stimuli for recordings can be provided to some extent within the classroom, for children young enough to need such structuring, but ultimately it is desirable for students to choose a time and place outside of class to do their recording. Animals, mechanical contraptions, science demonstrations, pantomimists—anything that moves—can serve in the structured situation. The shift from teacher-selected to student-selected stimuli can accompany a shift from isolated senses to interplay of senses. That is, first a student is asked to record only what he hears, or sees, or touches of what is presented in school, and then to record all his sensations somewhere away from school.

Students unable to write can dictate their verbalized sensations to the teacher or to older students. In fact, it might be better for any student who is concentrating on sounds or touch to close his eyes and dictate to a partner who would then trade places with him. The dictation itself can be a strong learning device, since it entails breaking the flow of speech sounds into words and other units; spelling, punctuation, and accuracy of quotation can then be gone over together by the partners. (This practice can be related in turn to recording dialogue.) Expedients have to be devised for somehow capturing events that happen too fast to keep up with otherwise. The problem is the same for someone recording sights and sounds as it is for someone playing stenographer; both are in a sense taking dictation. By reading and discussing their records, students can explore telegraphic and fuller styles, the best ways to capture sensations hurriedly, options of word choice, and the degree of dispensability of different parts of speech. They can also discuss the advantages of composing after the fact and the various ways of rewriting that would be required to make a record understandable and interesting to another audience.

In fact, a teacher can exploit recording for virtually anything he wishes to teach—linguistics, semantics, point of view, description, narrative. By varying the speed and conditions of the assignment, he can bring different linguistic structures under scrutiny. By asking several students to record at the same time and place, he can work with the different ways students name the same phenomena, differences in their perceptual selections and differences in their physical vantage points. If, just after a pantomime performance, the spectators write down what they think it was they witnessed, they can discuss their different interpretations and relate these differences to ambiguities in the acting and to idiosyncrasies of recording. Recordings made by the same student at the same place but at a different time can be compared also. If students are asked to spot personal judgments in their own and others' recordings, they become adept at separating physical fact from inferences and interposed attitudes—or at least at discovering the subtle interrelations of these things. They should be led to contemplate the way what we see is influenced by our wants, prior interests, and conventions—how concept influences percept.

Since the order of utterances is determined by the order of events, recordings are chronological, but in two ways. An active scene bombards the observer with an external order of events, whereas a still life tableau forces the observer to fall back on the order of his own body movements. That is, contrary to what composition texts say about static description, there is no such thing as *spatial* order. Only time can order in the physical world. The order of items in a still life description is determined by the observer's attentional sequence—either his movement in that space, the movement of his head and eyeballs, or the idiosyncrasies of his perceptual selections, which may be partly conceptual. In short, we have a record either of external events beyond the observer's control or of the observer's actions themselves.

Students ready to look inward somewhat can be asked to record, first, their internal sensations, then their flow of memories, then their flow of thoughts. Many young people, and adults, are unaware of what they are feeling, kinesthetically and emotionally, until they consciously turn attention inward to the organs and other parts of the body. Then they

notice little aches, itches, and muscular tensions, or emotions as mani-
fested by physical sensations. Next, using immediate surroundings as
stimuli to trigger past sensations, the student begins writing down trains
of memories and, eventually, trains of thought associations. Although
memories concern what happened and reflections concern what happens
or may happen, the *act* of remembering or reflecting is a part of what is
happening now, and like any other events of the present can be recorded
as it goes on. The gradual shift of focus inward is one curriculum progression; another is the sensations-memory-reflections sequence, which
mounts the abstraction ladder of symbolic activities.

The inner verbal system called soliloquy is really a mixture of currents, but by focusing attention on one of these currents we can make it
nearly exclude the others, temporarily. This happens naturally all the
time—as inner and outer events "call attention to themselves"; what the
teacher's assignment does is act as an outside influence that helps the
student tap these currents for their rich and individualistic materials.
Furthermore, a lot of the stream is actually subverbal or perhaps un-
conscious and does not really become soliloquy until an effort of attention
brings it to the word level.

Writing Scripts and Dialogues

Taking dictation, recording behavior, and improvising dramas and
discussions should all ease the way to play writing in two ways. One is
in training the eye to note behavior and the ear to note speech; the
other is in getting a sense of responsiveness and interplay among people.
Trying to write plays should further develop such faculties as well as
make the reading of plays a much more meaningful experience. What
I will outline here is a suggested sequence of assignments in dramatic
writing.

A good beginning is to invent a short, unbroken conversation between
two people, what I call a duologue. The point is to get something interesting going between the people without worrying too much about wrapping
up the ending in a big climax. (One kind of two-person drama is a
monologue spoken to someone who does not speak.) From this point of
departure the student progresses to a triadic relationship, which is
already a lot more difficult to handle, and then on to a longer scene that
mixes duets, trios, and quartets. He is encouraged to try soliloquies. He is
told to limit stage directions to what the audience can see and hear. This
is to prevent the amateur tendency to tell how characters feel and to
insert abstract information. A severer limitation is to write the script with
no stage directions, so that time, place, and circumstances must all come

through the dialogue. In any case, until the student can write a dialogue for several voices that is indeed dramatic, it seems a good idea to hold the play to one continuous scene. This can produce one-acters, and even if the student stops here he has learned a lot. The next step is to write a play of several scenes. This complexity brings on problems of plotting and selection that approach similar problems in narrative. Which action is to occur offstage and which on? How is the offstage action to be summarized for the audience? Pacing also becomes more difficult along with the effective juxtaposing of scenes of different times and places. Whatever the degree of complexity, it is important that the writer draw his characters, action, and setting from a world he has some knowledge of; otherwise he draws on all the movies and TV shows he has seen.

Writing Socratic dialogues can build a bridge from drama to essays of ideas. The student designates two voices as A and B and writes a dialogue between them about some topic he or the class has chosen. The topic might be something about what the class has been reading. This conversation is improvised straight off on paper for about a half hour. The purpose is to turn over a subject and get different points of view on it. Older students could work with three or four voices and afterwards rewrite the dialogue as an essay by merging the voices into one but without eliminating any worthwhile arguments. This conversion of dialogue into essay requires that a student fuse separate statements by grammatically synthesizing them. This process is parallel to the internalization I spoke of as occurring in real conversation. Doing this alone on paper presupposes a lot of oral experience. It asks, in effect, that the student bring out and put into play whatever points of view he has stored, without fear of contradicting himself. Then, in the essay, he assimilates the various arguments into a monological discourse, a feat which entails shifting his own point of view to a level of abstraction higher than that of any one of the arguments.

Another sequence, parallel, goes from collaborative to individual script writing. Before reaching the stage of simply sitting down and writing a play alone, a student should first be allowed to help a script evolve out of small-group improvisation. After improvising several versions of a situation, the group discusses and drafts together a script of their favorite version. This might be given to another group to perform.

Before passing on to the receptive activities, I think I should make it clear that the purpose of asking students to write in play form, or in any other literary form, is not to engender hordes of little creative writers. My concern is greater for a curriculum that helps semiliterate, nonverbal types of children than one that fosters the gifted. The very profound relationship that exists between literary and everyday discourse—some of which I hope I have demonstrated in this essay—is such that to work in one is to work in the other. Nearly all the assignments I am recommending have multiple goals. A student who writes a play is learning how to converse, to appreciate an art form, to understand himself, to describe, and, very generally, simply to write. Let's look at these goals a moment.

To begin with the last, creating a play script allows a young student to write a lot of colloquial speech at a time when he may not be ready to compose more formal sentences. He can write as people talk. Continuity and organization are relatively easy because the sequence of utterances need not be abstractly logical but can follow the familiar social give-and-take of conversation. And yet the writer is faced with the primary writing task of making sights out of sounds, of reproducing voice through orthography and punctuation. Writing dialogue is the best way to learn to punctuate. If it is clear that the script must enable someone else to read the lines as the author heard them in his head when he wrote them, then the author knows he must use typography as a set of signals indicating to a reader where the stresses and pauses are and how the intonation goes. This is what the breaking and punctuating of sentences on the page is all about anyway. The rules are merely an attempt to generalize the relations between sound, syntax, and sense. But no one ever has trouble punctuating orally; the problem is rendering speech on the page. Children who don't learn how to punctuate in twelve years of rules could learn in a few months by having other students *mis*read their own dialogues back to them. The problem is one of egocentrism: hearing in his own head the correct intonation and pauses of an utterance he is writing, the author doesn't realize that someone else is likely to impose a different reading unless he is guided by typographical cues. Overcoming such egocentrism requires, first, an awareness of what he is hearing himself, and then an awareness that the other person does not know what he knows. Both spelling and punctuation can be worked on by subgroups of students reading and diagnosing each other's dialogues—once the teacher has focused them, with some examples, on the real issues involved. A language teacher is not a proofreader and should never become one.

Stage directions are a combination of narrative and description. The referents are physical. Although the narrative part can follow chronological order and is central to the action, the description is intermittent and accessory, as is the case for description generally. Above all, therefore, it must be relevant and significant, well selected and well timed. A natural criterion is that the physical appearance of a character or a setting should relate to the action and to the author's purpose. What should be the order of items, and therefore of utterances, when telling how something looks when it does not move? This is a good task and one that goes beyond the logic of time.

All I will say about learning to converse through playwriting is that writing dialogue activates one's repertory of potential voices and gives practice in building conversations with these voices.

Understanding art and understanding oneself I want to take together and apply beyond drama, for the sake of a general educational principle, which is to let students write their own literature. Although one very reasonable argument for this principle is that students can often write better and more appropriate reading material for each other than is manufactured for them by some adult writers of primers, my case rests on a couple of more important beliefs. They are that a student who role plays the artist (1) comes to appreciate and understand the art form intuitively without needing teacher explanation and tedious vivisections and postmortems, and (2) that some of the benefits that accrue to the artist accrue to him. Anyone who has written some duologues and triologues, or one-acters, or a whole play is much more likely to grasp for himself what the dynamics is of a certain moment in Ibsen or Shakespeare, what the main vector is of a certain scene, or its purpose, why some scenes occur offstage and some on, how people's speech characterizes them, what the importance is of setting and objects, what a clumsy or expert exposition is, and so on. The same is true with fiction and poetry. Most inexperienced students take all the decisions of the artist for granted. In fact, they see no choice, only arbitrariness or inevitability. Appreciation of form comes only with a sense of the choices—from the selection of persona, locale, and events to who goes offstage when and what gesture accompanies which speech. When you yourself invent, you see all the choices, make decisions; the arbitrariness and inevitability of what professionals do disappears. It all begins to make sense. You are on the inside of the game, and it is more fun to play this way. When you discuss a professional play in class, you are motivated to talk about how the author says what happens by presenting what is happening. Because you know what he is doing, you know what he is saying.

The benefits an artist enjoys concern the exploitation and controlling of his fantasies for an objective connection and for self-knowledge. Fantasies are one kind of abstracting, and the purpose of abstracting is to reduce reality to something manageable. Children, like adults, make their way in the world and among their own feelings by creating some abstractions that help manage reality. They will fantasy anyway; all the teacher is asking them to do is shape some of these fantasies in words and forms which are public. An artist externalizes his fantasies, sells them for profit, and at the same time gets a chance to examine them and have them examined. All people seem to feel a vital need to find correspondences, "objective correlatives," between mind and world. Perhaps this is partly in order to get in touch with less conscious parts of themselves, but it is partly, I think, just to connect for its own sake. To plug inner experience into outside equivalents seems to be of profound importance for human beings. Otherwise it is difficult to account for the addiction both children and adults have for stories, in whatever medium. Instead of merely projecting *into* someone else's inventions, the artist projects his own. The advantage is greater personal accuracy and appropriateness of fantasy to feeling. One of the benefits to the student as artist, then, is creating symbols through which to correspond with the outside world, and by which he can learn about himself. Once externalized in public, i.e. impersonal, forms, ideas, and feelings can be dealt with, changed, and resolved. For less verbal children such expression may be more important than for the talented.

Creating fictions, imaginatively recombining real elements, is thinking. The fact that these elements may be characters, events, and objects does not make a literary construction less an act of thought than any other kind of abstraction. Art is simply a different *mode* of abstracting. It is a great mistake for the teacher to imagine an opposition between "creative" writing and idea writing. The ideas in plays and novels may not be named, as in exposition, but they are there. They are implicit in the selection, arrangement, and patterning of events and character. The art is to *embody* ideas. And the child's first grasping of ideas is through embodiments of them. A student writing a play automatically makes it a way of saying something; there has to be something determining his choices. Whereas recording grounds discourse in reality, inventing allows a student to recombine things in ways he has not witnessed and thus opens the realm of possibility. This is the precursor for advanced logic, which consists of permuting knowns so as to arrive at unknowns.

Reading

Of the three input activities two have already been dealt with above—listening and witnessing. When some students are improvising a drama or panel, or performing a play, the others are looking on. Recording, taking dictation, and interacting in conversation all develop alertness and receptivity. I need add only the important experience of listening to tapes and discs and watching films. Professional recordings and films of plays are of course an excellent way to bring alive dramatic literature, but I would recommend in particular the practice of playing a recording of a play, poem, or story while the students follow the text. This gives real voice to the words on the page and thus enables the student to *hear* meaning and emotion as well as pronunciation and the intonation patterns of both colloquial and literary discourse. Such tight binding of sound, sight, and sense should improve silent reading and comprehension of the text, strengthen the internalization of new language forms and vocabulary, and increase involvement with literature. In lieu of professional recordings, local tape recordings can be made by teachers, other adults, or talented students.

There is another kind of drama that has seldom been tapped for classroom use. It is the ceaseless production of court rooms, hearings, senate committee investigations, and actual panel discussions. These are not only dramatic in the general sense but also often downright theatrical. They illustrate beautifully the tight relation between interplay of roles and personalities and the dialectic of ideas. At the same time as they deal seriously with important ideas, they forcefully enact the dynamics of groups. I think that curriculum builders should make a great effort to obtain transcripts, tapes, and kinescopes of these real-life dialogues. These could be heard, seen, and read in conjunction with the performing and reading of dramatic literature. Students should understand clearly both the similarities and differences between everyday, spontaneous dialogues and composed, literary plays. Though the theater simulates real behavior, at some degree of remove, it also harmonizes, resolves, relates, and transforms it. While seeing the unreality of realism, the artifice of art, the student can at the same time appreciate the organic relevance of plays to life.

Reading a play alone should occur only after improvising and performing plays and should be interwoven with the writing of dramatic pieces and the witnessing of professional performances. Until a student has had the experience of hearing and seeing plays and being in them, an experience that enables him to bring the script alive in his imagination, the reading of plays is not very rewarding and creates unnecessary problems of incomprehension. The failure of most play teaching is due to this lack of preparation. The text of a play leaves the reader more on his own than most narratives, which describe, guide, and explain more. A script requires a lot of inference. On the page, a young reader doesn't "see" where X is standing when he is delivering a certain line, or who he is saying it to, or which actions are taking place concurrently. Nor does he "hear" the significant inflections or tones of voice. If this is so for modern plays, it is true *a fortiori* for Shakespearean texts, which have few stage directions. Generally, no narrator provides continuity between scenes or says what people are thinking or hints at their motives. A rough sequence, then, is from the boards to the book, but always returning to the boards (or film or tape) as often as possible.

Once the reading is launched, however, a more specific sequence is possible, the one outlined for the writing of plays. It goes from simple to complex but not by dint of extracting parts from plays. In fact, the idea is never to assign anything less than a complete play but to choose, in the beginning, whole short plays that in effect constitute the building blocks of larger, more complex plays, that is, to find works of dramatic literature that are monologue, duologue, or triologue unfolding continuously at one time and place. These are one-scene plays limited to very few voices and hence to a simpler psychological dynamics. From this point progression is toward increasing number of voices and relations, more complex orchestration of *groups* of voices, and increasing extension of the action in time and space. The farther flung a play—the more scenes it has occurring at different times and places, and the larger the cast—the more the play becomes narrative and expository. That is, plot becomes more important, interim action must be summarized, the relations of scenes made clear, the identities of new characters conveyed, and their relevance explained. Whereas the more here and now, the more dramatic.

If we include within drama a lot of poetry that purports to be a recording of persona voices speaking now—interior monologues, dramatic monologues, and duologues—we enlarge the repertory of whole short works. The test is whether they could be put on stage. Soliloquies like "Soliloquy of a Spanish Cloister," "Ode to a Nightingale," "The Love Song of J. Alfred Prufrock," and "Ulysses"; dramatic monologues like "My Last Duchess," "The Ballad of the Goodly Fere," and "To His Coy Mistress"; mixed interior and dramatic monologues like Henry Reed's "Naming of Parts"; duologues like "Lord Randall," "Ulysses and the Sirens," "Ann Gregory," Reed's "Judging Distances," and "West-Running Brook" all could be performed. So long as the poem presents the unintroduced, uninterrupted transcription of what some characters are saying at a certain time or place or in certain circumstances, it is dramatic. Many poems are difficult for students to understand simply because they do not expect drama in a poem and immediately assume that the voice they hear is the author's and that he is philosophizing. "My Last Duchess," which even my bright eleventh graders seldom understood on the page, would be very comprehensible if two people acted it out—one gesturing to a portrait and speaking about it while the other reacted with growing revulsion until he finally started prematurely down the stairs. In fact, some short stories are interior and dramatic monologues and differ from some of these poems only in being in prose. My point could best be made if the reader were to compare the text of "My Last Duchess" with that of Strindberg's play *The Stronger* and George Milburn's story "The Apostate," each of which has one speaker and one silent reactor. When a work is clearly dramatic, it should be taught as such, regardless of the genre under which it is classified. And a lot of literature that could *not* be performed is better understood on the page if the student is used to characterizing and situating voices and to shifting from one voice to another.

Let me adumbrate a possible sequence of play readings. The selections below are meant only to illustrate; I have chosen plays that adult readers might be familiar with rather than plays necessarily appropriate for young readers. Since I have not sifted a lot of short plays aimed at pre-adolescent readers, I do not know if good selections exist for them that could occupy the slots in the first half of this sequence. If not, I would say to let the students create their own equivalent literature. I do not include here any poems or short stories, but the reader can insert at the appropriate places some of the examples above or some of his own examples. The exact placement of interior monologue or soliloquy is difficult because it depends on the readiness of students to recognize internal discourse. Here I will assume a student reader old enough to understand soliloquy as a real phenomenon. The opening choice finesses this issue somewhat anyway, since Emperor Jones is childlike enough still to "think out loud" and to see outside what is really inside. Also, *Emperor Jones* is not a play that is strictly continuous in time, and admittedly this principle of plot expansion in time and space is sometimes at odds with the principle of moving from single voice to multiple voice. But I think any teacher will see that in establishing a sequence of readings these two principles are to be exploited only in the measure that they make a realistic pathway for the student; they are not to be adhered to absolutely.

Emperor Jones, Eugene O'Neill (A duologue that quickly becomes an extended soliloquy in which imagined creatures people the stage)

The Stronger, August Strindberg (A monologue spoken to a listener who reacts wordlessly)

Hello, Out There, William Saroyan (Begins as a solo that becomes a long duet that returns to solo. Man and girl duologue)

The Zoo Story, Edward Albee (A duologue between two men that lapses for long stretches into monologue)

Miss Julie, August Strindberg (A triangle of one man and two women but only two are together at a time. Essentially duologue of man and woman who lapse often into monologue. Dance interlude but duration is unbroken)

No Exit, Jean-Paul Sartre (A full-blown triangle of man and two women. Often duologue but always influenced by presence of third party. Dynamics of triadic group)

Electra, Sophocles (Mother-son-daughter story but actually consists of serial duologues between Electra and five others; occasional triologue; ranges from stichomythia to soliloquy and narrative monologue)

Candida, Bernard Shaw (Husband-wife-youth triangle but includes minor characters and spans a whole day; broken into scenes; two settings)

The Glass Menagerie, Tennessee Williams (A mother-son-daughter triad broken up by catalyst of fourth character; one setting but covers weeks or months; whole play is a memory soliloquy by the narrator, resembling *Emperor Jones*)

The Master Builder, Henrik Ibsen (Husband-wife-girl triangle, but this group interlocks via main character with another trio; several scenes but covers short period of time)

Macbeth, William Shakespeare (Complex of soliloquies, duologues and group dialogues, covering first a few hours then months and years)

A student who reads, and to some extent writes, his way through such a sequence is tracing the development of dramaturgy, not historically, but structurally and psychologically. Structurally because the earlier plays, while complete in themselves, feature solely and then in combination the components of which the later plays are made. Psychologically, because a sequence based on the changing interplay of voices can array the different dynamics of human interactions that occur as the number, sex, and kind of relationship change. Reading plays in some such order as this could increase the student's awareness, I believe, of the fundamental kinds of discourse and psychological relations that make up what we call a play. Thus certain plays read earlier may prepare students for certain other plays read later thereby obviating considerable analysis and explanation.

The principle of such an order is more important than the exact order itself. Form and dynamics are timeless and provide an entrée into plays of another era that might seem too remote to a present-day reader. Whereas a purely content approach may make it very difficult for a young person to relate to his own world the goings-on in Shakespeare or Ibsen, he can readily translate from their duets or triangles to those he is familiar with. I have often asked students to represent character inter-actions on the board with arrows or other graphic symbols. They always found this a reasonable request. There is something structural about both human emotions and human interactions. That is, you can replace the content of a feeling or the content of an exchange with another and something will still remain the same—something like the pitch, vibra-tion, or intensity of the feeling (whether it is love or hate, fear or elation) and, in interaction, something like the pattern of energy, the lines of force. We ride the momentum of a particular dynamic until another dynamic cuts across it. Once one is tuned into varieties of pitch and pace and lines of force, one is on to drama, because it is the intensities and vectors of energy that carry a play, and these affect the participants and the observers more than what the drama is about.

RHETORIC

Several teaching issues relate to all of the activities and methods which I have been dealing with up to this point. They concern general aspects of discourse. One of these is rhetoric.

For me *rhetoric* refers to the ways one person attempts to act on another, to make him laugh or think, squirm or thrill, hate or mate. Unlike other animals, the human baby cannot for some time do for itself. During the first months of utter helplessness and the following years of extreme dependence, the child must get others to do for it. Thus we learn at the outset of life the tremendously important art of manipulating other people. This is the genesis of rhetoric—and it begins before we learn to speak. Crying soon becomes a means of summoning the milk supply or the dry diaper. Later the rhetorical repertory of the child includes vomiting, holding breath, throwing temper tantrums, evacuating inappropriately, whining, wheedling—and obeying. Acting on others through words is merely one aspect of the larger rhetoric of behavior.

Now, although we are concerned here with acting on others through words only, the fact is that, as a specialization of general instrumental behavior, verbal rhetoric originates in mixture with other behavior—as on the stage—and only later, when we learn to monologue in writing, does it isolate itself. The guts of drama is rhetoric, people acting on each other; speech is featured but nonverbal influence is highly prized, to say the least. A play is a model of how the student, his parents, friends, and enemies do things to each other verbally and in conjunction with gesture, voice, and movement. In a play the communicants are "live," existential; the personalities behind the words are the most real, the intentions and ploys the most evident. Everything is *present*. Drama is the perfect place to begin the study of rhetoric. Confronted with a written monologue —a novel, essay, or treatise—a student deals with a phantom by comparison. An essay has a speaker who in turn has motives and ways of acting on his audience. But this action-at-a-distance will be much harder to recognize and respond to if the student has not been long accustomed, through experience with drama, to link words to speakers to motives. Reading, witnessing, and discussing plays will sensitize him to rhetoric, and he should also practice it himself, in his own voice and in invented voices, by improvising, writing, and performing dramas. Even if our student is destined to write nothing more than notes to the milkman, or to discourse only orally, he can at least learn to do these things effectively through a developed rhetoric and become aware that what is bombarding him through the mass media issues from people who have designs on him. Although we enter school already with a rhetoric, it is of course naive and drastically inadequate to later communication needs. The function of the school is to extend the rhetorical repertory and to bind messages so tightly to message senders that this relation will not be lost in transferring it to the page. What is too obvious to notice in conversation must be raised to a level of operational awareness that will permit this transfer.

STYLE

Closely related to how A acts on B through words is A's choice of diction, phrasing, sentence structure, and organization—his style. The best preparation for discriminating styles on the page is to become attuned to them in person. Reading is listening to somebody talk. This does not mean that we write in just the same way as we talk, but simply that writing is monologuing. In fact, the special qualities of writing are best understood when seen as changes in diction, phrasing, sentence structure, and organization made, precisely, in order to adjust to the loss of vocal and facial expression, gesticulation, feedback, collaboration, and the other characteristics of conversation. Ideally, as one reads he would hear a voice and conjure a person who would be uttering it. This person would be someone capable of saying such things in such ways. To teach style I would emphasize the continuity between dramatis personae in plays and the admittedly paler personae who are the authors of written monologues.

One is unlikely, however, to detect stylistic differences if one hears no more than one style, just as one is not likely to detect phonetic distinctions made in other languages but not in one's own. This is another reason why students should be exposed in the classroom to a wide range of voices, dialects, and life styles, and why they should role play different people. A style proceeds partly from a class and ethnic background, and partly from a role or stance, and partly from personal idiosyncrasy. Some of style is conditioned and some is a matter of changing wishes, as when a writer decides to take a debonair, foreboding, or satiric posture with a certain essay but not with another. Differences precede choice and choice precedes style. A student asked to take such and such a role in an improvisation realizes that he should try to "sound like" that persona. Writing dialogue requires differentiating the voices of various personae and applying the realistic criterion that words should match their speakers and the stances of the speakers. The educational principle involved here is that a thoroughgoing attunement to the styles of voices in the here-and-now makes it possible later to "hear" a style on the page. Also, out of a diverse dramatic experience the student can begin to develop choice, break through stereotyped conditioning, and create a voice that truly utters him.

52

THE DRAMA OF THE CLASSROOM

As for teaching language generally, a dramatic pedagogy is superior to an expository one. It seems terribly misguided to me to *tell about* something to students when they are *using* that something every day of their lives. As a school subject, language is unique in this way. In fact, it is truly language only when it *is* being used. It is not really a something at all; it is an action going on in somebody's head or between people. Words in a book are mere paper and ink until someone starts to read them. And he reads them only by virtue of a prior social activity. The expository approach would prepare textbooks and workbooks that either tell a student what he is already doing or tell him what he ought to be doing in his verbal behavior. Since this verbal behavior can be practiced in the same room in which it can be told or read about, the most sensible course, it seems to me, is to behave verbally and behave some more verbally about that behavior and thus modify and enlarge discourse in the ways the expository approach means to do (and in some ways doesn't mean to do). The prepared statements and exercises of textbooks never come at the right time to modify behavior; only something more extemporaneous can do that. To read and be told about, at one time and place, how language works and how we should best use it, then to try to discourse for real at another time and place . . . well, to make such an application and transfer presupposes an intellectual attainment that could only be the end not the means of an education. Correction and enlightenment "take" best when they come right in midtask, when the knowledge is just what one needs to know at that moment.

Besides being inefficient and irrelevant, exposition is inhumane. It is dull. In other subjects it may to some extent be unavoidable if the subject is a corpus of facts which the student cannot know any other way. But the facts and possibilities of discourse can be known in another way, one more akin to how the student has been learning language and to how he will be using it out of school, except that this dramatic method can be used with a consciousness and deliberateness denied to the home and the marketplace.

As much as teachers may often wish that they could ignore, eliminate, or stylize into innocuousness the sociality of the classroom, they neither

53

should do so nor can they. Ultimately a student, or adult for that matter, is more interested in his relation to other people than he is in a subject, because psychic survival and fulfillment depend on what kind of relation one works out with the social world. Since some life drives are at stake, no student is going to forsake this interest no matter how tough the discipline; the teacher can't control the student's mind. He will get interested in the subject to the extent that he can make it relevant to his current needs. Instead of creating constant tension between the social motives of the student and his own motive to teach the "subject," the teacher would do better to acknowledge that his own intellectual pursuits are framed by dramatic relations between him and the world, and to recognize that this must be true for his students as well. Since discourse is ultimately social in origin and in function, it seems a shame to fight those forces that could be put to such excellent use in teaching the subject.

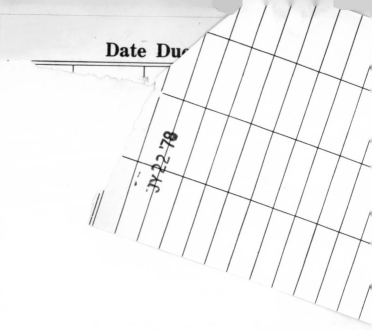